The End Of The Road

Stephanie Ray

BookLeaf Publishing

India | USA | UK

Made with ❤ on the BookLeaf Publishing Platform
www.bookleafpub.in
www.bookleafpub.com

Dedication

To my Lomie, Forever and Always

Preface

We try until we can't lie to ourselves anymore.
-STEPHANIE RAY

Acknowledgements

1. Sour Patch Kid

I am sour
I used to be sweet
my love was empowered
delusional dream
joyous desire
pain overlooked
never enough
always trying to impress
you were never satisfied
your needs weren't met
and yet you stayed
I still wonder why

was it wasted time
cynical mind

2. A Thought

Do you think of me as I think of you.
Never just out of the blue.
Intentionally as our love was true.
Can you
See it?
Can we retrieve it?
Am I delusional to believe it?

I love you and my heart aches to tell you

3. Soap

3

The soap dish always ends up full
The hand soap never bear
These aren't things you refill yourself
 But somehow they are always there

Maybe that's love
Maybe it's not
But one thing I know for sure
That's how you show somebody you care you

4. Delete This Like all the Others You Archived

The things I wrote for you
Half of them deleted
Things I wish I said
Back when you believed me

God how I miss you
I just wish to kiss your lips
And you be the one to hold me
As the worlds a sinking ship

5. For gods sake

When will you believe me?
When is my truth seen
Nothings right if it comes from me
According to you at least

Why come back?
Why not just leave me the fuck alone?
What would you be if you didn't accuse me so much

Give me peace
For gods sake give me peace or let me be
Let me be if you don't love me

This isn't love
The way you speak
Have I even had a say?
Check your speech

You want truth
I've given you honesty
You don't want it
Then you don't want me
Just leave me be to grieve

6. Eventually

Eventually I'll stop calling
The words will be too much
I will see my worth
And you've given me none

Eventually I'll stop trying
For love is not enough
I will no longer cry
And you will be what?

Eventually I'll manage
Even if it rips my heart in two
Eventually I'll stop crying for me and you

7. Still Unchanged

Sad eyes
White lies
No surprise
She's crossing lines
Raised voice
Erase for choice
Still weak
Still seek
Not enough growth to conceal my heat

Back door dirty pics
Hands around my neck intense
Bedroom sheets lay me down
Beat me till I'm blue and drown
Kitchen cooking
Utensils laid
across my face intentions made
Hands to hold
Fists to throw
Broken glasses
Punctured nose
Music played
Words of hate

It's all my fault
I'll take the blame

8. Unfound

Everything makes me think of you and at times I wish I
remembered nothing.
All this heart break and pain I'll give you a piece.
Too many events have unfolded.
Too many things to unsee.
Too many things have been said.
Can we unbleed?
Love seeping out.
Never leave you in drought.
We always bounce back
But truth is I'm unfound.
I'm different now.

9. Not My Home

This place is not my home
A foreign place I once knew
A Dystopian escape
All at once a woe
This place is not my home
A box of memories I cannot visit
Each time I do flood gates glisten
No happy reminiscence
So you claim
Looks like we are finally on the same page

10. Enough

We lead different lives now
It's sad they used to be the same
You fell down the rabbit hole
And never looked to reclaim

I've begged and pleaded
All you refute
You're caught up in it refuse to move
I can't stay with you
I have to move forward
Better things ahead
Less pain to endure

Why stay stuck?
What's in it for you?
4 minutes of torture equals 7 years of pain
But it's still not enough, no
You must keep going
7 more years you'll give instead of letting go?
7 more years of this is what is in your plan

A baby isn't what you want
or so that's what you claim
Except you picked out the donor

and were there for the day
Positive test had you smiling equally to mine
Or was that my own delusion in spite?
Are we that easily left in the dust to your anger?
Easily tossed away when mad?
You become a product of what you know
The lack of effort stabs

I can't
I won't
For the sake of something bigger than me
Bigger than us

You claim you wouldn't want this for your child but you
are fine doing this to me?
Who have I been married to?
Where did my wife go
I think I've been searching for her for years and I can't
find her
When is it time to let go
When is it all too much
When is enough enough

11. Please

Please don't work against me
Please god let her see
We can both escape this
If you work with me

My love has not faded
It still wavers strong
Your love is somewhere in there
Remember when we were one

I don't want to hurt you
I always wanted better than this
How did our love become twisted
Why do you refuse to see
I would go to the end of the earth for you
I'd give up me

12. Bound

The thing that bound us
Did you even care?
I'd do anything for you
Except leave you bare
Till death do us part
A promise I want to keep
Through the good and the bad
Who knew it'd get this deep

There is still a chance right?
Can we come back from this?
I want my family whole again
I deserve forgiveness

13. Slipping

15

Trying to spare myself but running out of reasons why I
should
They all disrespect me and think I'll be good
Why do I keep trying
The hole is deep
I keep on digging but I'm slipping slick feet

1. Nobody

Nobody sees my heart
Nobody understands my pain
When the love of my life refuses to change
The hate that I take
Your unfiltered rage
Tears me apart
Day.
By.
Day.

2. You

Who is making it difficultt?
Why always do the most?
I said keep it simple
For you I left it all
It's me you torture without even a call
You can't let go without getting a jab
You know I am weak
You know how to break me down

I'm trying to play nice
I left it all the same
You are the one acting in spite
While my eyes rain
Did your love exist???
My love still looks to you
Through the torture and the deceit
I still think of you

For you I only give
What you did through this wasn't for us
I must be crazy
To consider you in all this
Through the torture you've caused
No cat and mouse game for me

I want peace

Have whatever you need

It's always you I was thinking of while you think to
maltreat

3. Is it me that has to walk away?

I'm not suppose to be crying today.
It's not scheduled, unplanned
I can't help it when
I read your messages again
I pick all the dandelions in the yard
Just to blow them out with the same wish.
One that you'll treat me right
And I'll get to come home to you again
I miss you all the time
Especially at night
When I want to be held close
And there's nothing beside

How can I love someone
Who treats me this way
Who thinks it's okay to stay the same
What do I have to do
To make things change

Is it me that has to walk away?
I've begged on my knees
I've given everything I have
I have nothing left and for more you still ask

4. Too Far

I bite my nails down to the quick
A bad habit you always said I'd never kick
My day begins and ends with tears
I don't ask for them, they are just here
I found kindness in other people
Something you could never give me
I'm a new alcoholic
You're an outlaw land
Lime light
Shine bright
Don't take my peace tonight
I'm scared
Too much to share
Overbear
Blood shed another night
Endless yelling sleepless fight
Packing and moving
monotonous task
Sit on the porch, think of the past
All moments spent apart
Can we get these moments back or has the monster gone
too far?
I'm a thief
Is this my karma

Repayment for my sins
Endless trauma
Love I don't deserve
Something never received
I'll pay for a lifetime
What this took from me
Gritted teeth
Jaw clenched
Never before do I remember this
Revisit memories
Ones that hurt
Thrusting just like you deserve
Black eye
Strong cheeks
Hit upon the weak
I guess our love wasn't meant to be

5. Wading

Has it all been a lie?
Who hurt me this deep
Can I recover
I am wading weak
The eyes never dry
Your words cut mind
You don't care what you wreak
You want me to be six feet underneath
Misery speaks

I've learned to drown out the noise
Don't lock me inside
I must escape
There's no where to hide
The wakes are crashing
Waters chopping too dark to see
I keep wading even when weak

6. Beggars can't be Choosers

I begged for years
A night on the town
Never easy to get you out
Look at you moving with ease
You go out without a second guess or worry.

Family adventures?? Your down for the count
At least when it came to my side of grounds
Now look at you out and about
Seeing family talking non-stop
What was it with me?
I'm a lost cause.
At least that's what you claimed

Never good enough
Never tried with me, never tried to see
Everything's an issue if it's coming from me.

Who were you?
No damsel in distress.
Just someone who tells me I failed the test
What did you gain
Was the love even real
How can you feel good about the way you made me

feel?

I'll never understand
But I'll always try
That's what happen when loves in the eyes
They see things
You always overlooked
I cry in the shower
While you have me blocked
Making things easy
But you don't stop

I love you
I miss you
I want my life back
If there is even any life to be had

7. Can you picture it?

That night never left me
A new identity in the light
It buried me alive
It burrowed deep inside

Why do you push me until I break?
What is it that you want?
What's left to take?

One year since I lost you
One year but I still grieve
You're someone I prayed for
Something I can't leave

My life reduced to boxes
The love already gone
For you at least
Your words haunt me
8 years no dream
Recipes pulled
My clothes moved to a different closet
Everything yours I want nothing deposited

I hope to find you in another life

One where you are kind with your words and you don't
run but rather embrace
Where you see all that I offer and bring to the table with
grace
You boldly tell me all I've done to better you
Are you picturing this reality, too?

8. Unphased

I'm unphased
Your words cut deep but I'm still unbothered
I've heard them on repeat
No touchdown
Just a tyrant solider
Cry as I bake
This is why I don't try
You call me fake
As I still find compassion inside
These moments you take

It's all my fault
I'm a narcissist
I can't bare a child
I'll never have a kid
it would never survive
You lied to me
You lied to yourself
Bitch
Whore
Raped slut
The kindness makes me melt

It's alright

I'll take the blame
I know what I brought
Now I'm walking away
Claim it's all you
At night I still cry
Because I really cared
While you spread lies
Spin the narrative, never tell the truth
It's what you've always done
I gave it my all
You've won.
Where is your trophy?
What prize do you get??
Is it everything you imagined???
No pride did you neglect

This is how you spend your nights
8 year detriment, Talking shit
What will you do when I'm gone
Who will be to blame for it then

Meet yourself in the mirror
You couldn't face the truth
That's why you blame
No accountability you take

I've owned it all.

It's all my fault
I'll leave and be fine
Knowing I gave it my all
At least you can't say I didn't try. 💔